little book of

MiLAN
style

For Dominic

I'd like to thank my editor Heather Boisseau for her creative input and overall clarity; Silvia Signorini, Giovanna Sessi-Knott and Gianna Rechichi for their input, and David Scinto, Natalia Farran and Lucia Graves for their feedback.

First published in 2024 by Welbeck
An Imprint of HEADLINE PUBLISHING GROUP

1

Cataloguing in Publication Data is available from the British Library

ISBN 978 1 80279 783 1

Printed and bound in China by Leo Paper

HEADLINE PUBLISHING GROUP
An Hachette UK Company
Carmelite House
50 Victoria Embankment
London EC4Y 0DZ

www.headline.co.uk
www.hachette.co.uk

LAIA FARRAN GRAVES

little book of

MiLAN
style

WELBECK

CONTENTS

iNTRODUCTiON

Milan, Italy's fashion capital, is a bewitching city bursting with impeccable style. Whether it's the colour of a gelato, the sound of a roaring Vespa or the inviting smell of a freshly made espresso, style is everywhere – and fashion its embodiment. Where else but in Italy have the police force and the *carabinieri* been dressed by Fendi, Armani and Valentino? They also, of course, drive bulletproof Alfa Romeos and, on special occasions, Lamborghinis.

For centuries, the people of Italy have stood out for their sartorial splendour and rich heritage. From masterpieces by artists such as Sandro Botticelli (c.1445–1510) and Leonardo da Vinci (1452–1519) to the first ever operas, dating back to the 1600s, elegance runs through every aspect of their culture.

With Milan as one of the four fashion epicentres in the world, alongside Paris, New York and London, this unique carefree confidence and appreciation of quality over quantity defines an intoxicating aesthetic, one which is quintessentially Italian and revered the world over.

"I don't believe in good taste."
Gianni Versace

A glamorous Versace black dress is worn by Gigi Hadid in Versace's Autumn/Winter 2023 show, which took place in Hollywood.

Overleaf: Milan's Galleria Vittorio Emanuele II, with its spectacular four-storey double arcade, is the oldest shopping centre in Italy.

chapter 1

ĭTALY'S GOLDEN AGE

Following the Second World War, Italy experienced a period of prosperity and economic growth referred to by economists as "the Italian economic miracle" (*il miracolo economico italiano*). Television and radio slowly became part of daily life and Fiats, Vespas and Lambrettas were all the rage. The *Sanremo Music Festival, Eurovision*'s precursor, was in full swing, producing hit after hit (including Domenico Modugno's "Volare" in 1958 and Tony Renis' "Quando, Quando, Quando" in 1962), with tradition and innovation coming together, once again, to produce excellence. In the 1980s, the "Made in Italy" label was introduced, an accolade that became synonymous with luxury and quality craftsmanship. It covered what is known as the "Four A" sectors: *Agroalimentare* (food), *Arredamento* (furniture), *Automobili* (automobiles) and *Abbigliamento* (clothing). This universally recognized trademark not only stands for high quality and tradition, but also embodies a confident lifestyle that is timeless and elegant. So much so that the Institute for the Protection of Italian Manufacturers (*Istituto per la Tutela dei Produttori Italiani*), among others, set out to protect the label in 1999, with the Gucci company serving as its regulator under the Italian government.

> ## 'La semplicità è l'ultima sofisticazione.'
> **Leonardo da Vinci**
> *(Simplicity is the ultimate sophistication.)*

From Giorgio Armani to Ermenegildo Zegna, some of the most celebrated fashion designers in the world have come

Made In Italy

from Italy. With ateliers firmly rooted in Italian soil, their continued success can be attributed to talent, handed-down wisdom and choice of excellent materials.

During the 1950s, for example, Fendi reworked fur, treating it as they would any other fabric, developing ground-breaking techniques that combined *savoir faire* with modernity. Then, in 1966, they also dyed fur for the first time and during the seventies Fendi developed new practices, which involved cutting fur and overlapping it, shaving it, embellishing it and even knitting it – techniques that were revolutionary at the time. Another luxury fabric often selected by Italian designers is silk. Gianni Versace worked with the most talented printers worldwide to produce some of his most iconic silk prints, a process which could take up to eight months to complete, producing outstanding results. They

Audrey Hepburn and Gregory Peck starring in the romantic comedy *Roman Holiday*, 1953, for which Hepburn won an Academy Award for Best Actress.

The term *paparazzi* originates from the name of the character
"Paparazzo" – a ruthless photographer, played by Walter Santesso,
in Federico Fellini's masterpiece *La Dolce Vita* (1960).

were showcased in his Spring/Summer 1992 show, among
others, in a presentation that became known for its strong
designs and would change the way these were perceived and
utilized. The process would begin with a sketch, stencilled
onto a piece of paper. On a screen print, one by one, different
colours were applied by hand – each taking 20 minutes or
so – with a tenth of a millimetre between them. The prints
had between eight and approximately 20 colours each and
would be produced in 40-metre batch lengths, which would
make about 10 short dresses. These were so successful that
they were copied everywhere, something the designer saw as
a form of flattery.

From clothing to accessories, another beautiful material
for which Italian fashion is famed is its unique premium

Over 3,000 movies have been filmed at Rome's Cinecittà Studios, which were founded in 1937 by then Prime Minister Benito Mussolini.

leather, notably its highest-grade skin. Known for its full grain, because it is removed from the hide's outermost layer, this character-filled skin isn't sanded and therefore remains textured. Produced in Italy, it is mostly tanned with vegetable substances, such as tree bark, fruit and plants, using traditional methods passed down through generations of artisans. It can take up to 60 days for an expert master tanner to complete the process, depending on the finishes selected. A thinner top grain leather – a less expensive hide that has been smoothed and coated – is also sometimes used on accessories such as shoes, given its malleability. In 2006, the then Gucci Creative Director Frida Giannini introduced its *"Guccissima"* leather (meaning "the most Gucci"). This cherry-picked luxurious Italian leather was now also beautifully embossed with the timeless interlocking "double G" logo.

Today, the "Made in Italy" movement is committed to preserving Italy's culture and expertise, adopting sustainable production wherever possible. Projects such as Silvia Venturini Fendi's *Hand in Hand* are dedicated to supporting local artisans and maintaining their heritage. For this enterprise, ateliers from each of Italy's 20 regions created an iconic Fendi "Baguette" handbag (first launched in 1997), based on their personal interpretations of it. The first commission was a vegetable-tanned leather bag with no seams, made by skilled workers from Peroni, which appeared in Fendi's Autumn/Winter 2020 catwalk show. A further "Hand in Hand Baguette" was made in Veneto, where specialists at Bevilacqua created a jacquard version with a rich floral motif, using eighteenth-century looms (a process so labour-intensive that only a few centimetres were made each day). Equally delightful was the handbag made in Perugia by the family business Giuditta Brozzetti which is based in the extraordinary Church of Saint Francis of the Women. Here, ancient weaving techniques were used on precious looms to create a design featuring a horse, a peacock, a unicorn and a dove in bright royal blue and contrasting white. As Silvia Venturini Fendi explained: "Each bag is unique, because the imperfections inherent to handmade craftsmanship are what express intrinsic beauty. Fashion often focuses on the designer, and I think it's time that we celebrate the community of artisans behind these amazing creations."

Another initiative devised to honour tradition is the Circular Hub, spearheaded by Gucci in 2023, designed to champion a fully interconnected "Made in Italy" business model that not only supports local production and its excellent standards, but also protects the environment and overall social impact of the country's luxury manufacturing, including supply chains.

Actress Claudia Cardinale is seen here at the Sorelle Fontana Studios in Rome during a fitting.

LA DOLCE VITA

During Italy's post-war economic boom, the film industry flourished and Hollywood became mesmerized by Italian style. Despite being heavily bombed during the war, the legendary Roman motion picture studios *Cinecittà* (Cinema City) were eventually rebuilt and able to open their doors once again. This impressive "dream factory" is still Europe's largest, spreading over 400,000 square metres (1,312,336 ft), and containing 300 dressing rooms and offices.

Italian neorealism films, a genre that explored the poverty and hardship of the time, broke internationally, followed in the 1950s and '60s by more commercial movies, many of which were American productions. Attracted by low labour costs and subsidies, Hollywood began to shoot there, and because Italian law stated that proceeds from the pictures had to remain in the country, these profits were reinvested into further blockbusters. Soon, glamorous British and American stars were descending upon Rome's hotel-lined Via Veneto and the studio became known as "Hollywood on the Tiber".

It was an incredibly prolific period in movie history that produced spectacular material – from historical, epic "sword and sandal" flicks (*Ben-Hur*, 1959, starring Charlton Heston, *Quo Vadis*, 1951, with Peter Ustinov and Sophia Loren as an uncredited extra, and *Cleopatra*, 1963, featuring Elizabeth Taylor and Richard Burton), to romantic comedies (*Roman Holiday*, 1953, starring Audrey Hepburn and Gregory Peck) and legendary Spaghetti Westerns (*A Fistful of Dollars*, 1964, with Clint Eastwood in the leading role).

One of the most influential film directors of all time, Federico Fellini, on set at Cinecittà Studios.

Made In Italy

"Life is a combination of magic and pasta."

Federico Fellini

It was also during this time that Italian photographers began targeting the glitterati (Ava Gardner, Brigitte Bardot, Audrey Hepburn and Michelangelo Antonioni, to name but a few) by following them day and night on scooters, holding cameras with flashing bulbs to obtain sensationalist pictures that could be sold to the press. Fellini's *La Dolce Vita* (1960), a movie that has immortalized this golden era, tells the story of a tabloid journalist that takes place over seven days in Rome. In the movie, this leading press photographer is called *Paparazzo*, a character Fellini based on the unscrupulous snapper Tazio Secchiaroli (known as an "urban fox", the "*volpe di Via Veneto*"). The name stuck, and the rest, as they say, is history.

An early Valentino men's fashion show, Autumn/Winter 1990, displays the exquisite elegance for which the designer has become famous.

ALTA MODA COSTUME DESIGNERS

As the movie industry provided a window into Italian life, its actors became unofficial ambassadors for the "Made in Italy" movement. Behind the scenes, costume designers worked closely with the film companies to produce the most sensational wardrobes, curating a chic style and a mystique that attracted audiences worldwide.

Among these designers were the Fontana sisters (*Sorelle Fontana*) – Zoe Fontana (1911–1978), Micol Fontana (1913–2015) and Giovanna Fontana (1915–2004). Born in Parma's Traversetolo, they worked in their mother's dressmaking workshop (a business inherited from her grandmother), until they moved to Rome, where they furthered their skills working as tailoring apprentices and seamstresses. In 1943 they founded their *Alta Moda* studio in Via Liguria and their big break came in 1949, when the actress Linda Christian married fellow screen idol Tyrone Power wearing one of their dresses. Dubbed "the Wedding of the Century", it was a huge affair that took place in Rome's Basilica di Santa Francesca Romana, with up to 8,000 fans waiting outside. The fine dress, crafted from embroidered satin, had three-quarter length sleeves and a high neckline buttoned up to the collar. It also displayed a very long train and a matching Juliet cap with a delicate, long veil attached to it. Later that day, the happy couple were received by Pope Pius XII, head of the Roman Catholic Church.

The "Made in Italy" slogan as seen on a T-shirt from Dolce & Gabbana's Spring/Summer 2022 fashion show.

Anita Ekberg and Marcello Mastroianni in a scene from Fellini's 1960 film *La Dolce Vita*, which won an Oscar for Best Costume Design.

Overnight, *Sorelle Fontana Alta Moda SRL* became a couture powerhouse, with Zoe designing, Giovanna managing the business and Micol (nicknamed "the pigeon" because of her frequent trips to the US) acting as the face of the brand. They designed Myrna Loy's wardrobe in *That Dangerous Age* (1949), worked with celebrated American costume designer Edith Head on *Roman Holiday* (1953) and dressed Ava Gardner for *The Barefoot Contessa* (1954). They also produced the first uniforms for *Alitalia*'s cabin crew (1947–1964) and were one of the design houses to participate in the very first Italian *Alta Moda* fashion show staged in Florence in 1951, challenging the French competition.

Sorelle Fontana Alta Moda SRL was sold in 1992 to an Italian financial group, but the Fontana sisters' contribution had already left an indelible mark in the history of Italian style. Two years later, in 1994, the Micol Fontana Foundation was set up in Rome, housing a rich archive of their many creations. Others can be seen in Paris (at the Louvre museum) and in New York (at the Guggenheim and The Metropolitan Museum of Art).

Piero Gherardi (1909–71) was another highly influential set and costume designer who worked closely with Federico Fellini, imagining the costumes for *La Dolce Vita* and the fantasy drama 8½, both of which awarded him an Oscar. He had the extraordinary ability to set a mood through his designs and is famous for his emblematic outfits, including *La Dolce Vita* star Anita Ekberg's strapless black gown with high leg splits, which marked the dawn of a new era in celluloid.

iTALiAN iCONS

ELSA SCHiAPARELLi

Born in Rome into an aristocratic family descended from the Medicis, Elsa Schiaparelli (1890–1973) was a hugely influential fashion designer, artist and poet. A contemporary and rival of Coco Chanel, whom she referred to as "that milliner", Schiaparelli's unique avant-garde conceptual designs have stood the test of time. Her vision of the Dada and surrealist movements was particularly innovative and she enjoyed pushing thematic boundaries as well as experimenting fearlessly with unusual materials such as cellophane, metal and plastic. In 1922, she moved to Paris and was inspired by the French fashion designer Paul Poiret, with whom she struck a strong friendship. Her fame skyrocketed in 1927 when she created a *trompe l'oeil* sweater for herself, featuring a black and white bow that formed an optical illusion. It was described by *Vogue* as "a masterpiece" and prompted the designer to open her own couture house, in which she combined haute couture with sportswear. Her vision aligned with the work of artists such as Jean Cocteau (they designed a linen jacket together in 1937, with gilded metallic thread embroidery, beads and paillettes embellished with the shape of a woman stroking the waist of the wearer) and Salvador Dalí, whose collaborations became particularly era-defining. Schiaparelli's first project with Dalí was a compact powder case that looked like a rotary telephone (1935). They went on to create her famous lobster-decorated dress (1937),

A stunning Schiapparelli silk organdie strapless purple dress, worn with matching gloves and a navy pleated overskirt, was featured in *Vogue* on April 15, 1951.

Italian Icons

famously worn by socialite Wallis Simpson, as well as a high-heeled shoe hat (1937) and the padded skeleton dress (1938) for her *Le Cirque* collection, combining black silk crêpe with plastic zips. The pair – always blurring the lines between art and fashion – also designed a see-through plastic collar crawling with metal bugs (1938).

Schiaparelli decided to introduce shocking pink to her colour palette, a hue that became her signature shade, consolidating her eccentric persona. Her creative legacy continues to inspire today's designers and Maison Schiaparelli still offers bold and original fashion to an eclectic, alternative and very stylish clientele.

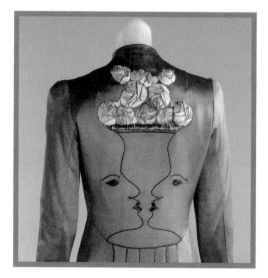

Above: Elsa Schiaparelli's love of fantasy is exemplified in this beautiful coat, made in 1937, with rayon, silk and gilded metallic thread embroidery.

Opposite: A lobster dress featured in Schiaparelli Spring/Summer 2017 collection, 80 years after the original version was worn by Wallis Simpson.

EMILIO PUCCI

Born in Naples to a Florentine aristocratic family, Emilio Pucci – the Marquis of Barsento (1914–92) – was a keen sportsman and a member of the 1934 Italian Olympic ski team, through which he obtained a skiing scholarship to attend Reed College in Oregon, US, in exchange for forming and coaching their first ski team. Having graduated, he returned home to find a government letter ordering him to serve in the armed forces by joining the Italian Air force.

While at Reed College, Pucci began to take an interest in fashion and designed the team's ski uniform, but it was after the Second World War, in 1947, when his career took off in earnest: one of his streamlined creations – a hooded ski outfit spotted on the slopes of Zermatt – was photographed for *Harper's Bazaar*.

Referred to as the "Prince of Prints" by the press, his use of patterns and swirly shapes in vibrant, bold colours created a unique aesthetic increasingly admired worldwide. His choice of fabrics – stretched silk jersey in particular – were also well received because they supported the newly-empowered modern woman by providing her with comfort and plenty of movement. In 1950, Pucci opened a boutique in Capri and during this time received the Neiman Marcus Award (in Dallas) and the Burdines Sunshine Award (in Miami). He also designed the uniforms for Braniff International Airways between 1965–73, at the height of the glamorous golden age of air travel, the strapline on the airline's advert reading "*The*

Italian Icons

Bright colours and a sixties silhouette were key elements in Pucci's Spring/Summer 2023 catwalk show.

Above: Pucci's Spring/Summer 2011 show was a seventies-inspired, elegant collection with a carefree Mediterranean feel.

Opposite: The luxurious and sophisticated Spring/Summer 2011 Pucci collection, designed by Peter Dundas, was a star-studded affair.

"Gaiety is one of the most important elements I brought to fashion. I brought it through colour."

Emilio Pucci

end of the plain plane". Soon he had a jet set following that included celebrities such as Elizabeth Taylor, Marilyn Monroe (who was buried in her favourite pale green Pucci dress), Jackie Kennedy and Sophia Loren. Between 1963 and 1972, Pucci was also a member of the Italian Parliament.

Pucci's unique ability to merge art and fashion and his explosive kaleidoscopic approach to colour has rendered his work timeless and loved through generations. During the 1990s, his daughter, Laudomia Pucci, took over the business as guardian of his heritage, guiding the company as image director and kickstarting a *puccimania* revival. And in 2009, when Beyoncé wore one of his dresses (black with a boatneck, to President Obama's inauguration ceremony), the *New York Times* proclaimed, "Pucci is relevant again."

In April 2000, LVMH (the French luxury conglomerate formed from the 1987 merger of Louis Vuitton and manufacturers of champagne and cognac Moët et Chandon and Hennessy) acquired 67 per cent of the Pucci company, and then in 2021, after roles at Dior and Louis Vuitton, Camille Miceli was appointed artistic director of the Maison, a position she fully embraced, celebrating its daring, psychedelic prints in particular.

A Pucci ski outfit, in a striking blue and green colourway, is worn by a model in 1969.

MARCELLO MASTROIANNI

The son of a carpenter, Marcello Mastroianni (1924–96) is widely considered one of the most renowned actors in the history of Italian cinema. His career began when he was just 14 and appeared as an uncredited extra in *Marionette* (1939). After several small acting roles, he played one of the main characters in *Atto di accusa* (1951) and soon afterwards got the leading role (a playboy tabloid reporter) in Federico Fellini's satirical comedy-drama, *La Dolce Vita* (1960), starring Anita Ekberg. In *8½* (1963), he played a filmmaker with writer's block, in a performance that showcased his compelling acting skills and his ability to portray complex characters – making him a symbol of the Italian New Wave of cinema. In addition, both of these films received an Academy Award for Best Costume, thanks to Piero Gherardi, who envisioned a glamorous debonair style with tailored suits, shirts, ties and designer sunglasses, modelled effortlessly by Mastroianni. During his fruitful career Mastroianni worked in 147 films and starred alongside Brigitte Bardot, Sophia Loren, Yves Montand and Jack Lemmon. He also received a number of international prizes, including two BAFTAs, two Best Actor Awards at the Venice and Cannes film festivals, two Golden Globes and three Academy Award nominations.

Mastroianni's suave charm and impeccable acting skills defined Italian cinema, and off-screen his style became as memorable as on film. Always looking sharp, his debonair flair made him the perfect poster boy for the splendour of the time.

Marcello Mastroianni and Anita Ekberg co-starred in
Federico Fellini's *La Dolce Vita*, 1960, an iconic film
that encapsulates the spirit of this golden era.

Between 1954 and 1994, Mastroianni and Sophia Loren became a household on-screen couple. They appeared in eight movies together.

SOPHIA LOREN

During the 1950s and '60s, Sophia Loren was the embodiment of Italian glamour. From figure-hugging designer ballgowns to casual beachwear, her fashion sense and sensuous style became synonymous with the elegance associated with her native country's golden era. Her story, however, is one of "rags to riches". Born Sofia Villani Scicolone in Rome in 1934, she grew up in poverty during the Second World War, but her striking looks, determination and talent led to her becoming one of the most celebrated actresses in the world.

Her contribution to cinema include performances in films such as *La Ciociara* (*Two Women*, 1960), in which she played a mother protecting her young daughter from the atrocities of war, and for which she won an Academy Award for Best Actress (she was the first actress to win an Oscar for a foreign language film) and *Yesterday, Today and Tomorrow* (1963), a comedy divided into three storylines co-starring Marcello Mastroianni, which won the Academy Award for Best Foreign Language Film, securing her position in Hollywood (where she had signed a contract with Paramount Pictures in 1958). Loren received a second Oscar, an Honorary award, in 1991. When she was just 15, she met the Italian film producer Carlo Ponti, who was 22 years her senior, and married him in 1966. They had two boys and were together until his death in 2007.

Beyond her acting career, drawing on her own experiences of a difficult childhood, Loren also took on many philanthropic and humanitarian causes she was truly passionate about, including the role of Goodwill Ambassador for the United Nations Development Programme (UNDP) in 1999.

Italian Icons

Above: Sophia Loren and Eleonora Brown in the film
La Ciociara (*Two Women*), 1960, for which Loren
received an Academy Award for Best Actress.

Opposite: Natural beauty Sophia Loren, photographed
in London, wearing a stunning shimmery dress.

WALTER ALBINI

Fashion designer Walter Albini (1941–83) is one of Italy's great unsung heroes. A colourful character, sporting an eccentric dandy aesthetic, he is often compared to the likes of Yves Saint Laurent and Halston. His unique forward-thinking vision, beyond the sketch pad, paved the way for future creatives.

Having studied at Turin's *Istituto d'Arte, Disegno e Moda* (where he was the only boy in the entire school), he became a skilled fashion illustrator for Italian magazines and newspapers, before moving to Paris to further his career. Once there, he met industry giants including Coco Chanel and Krizia's Mariuccia Mandelli, who asked him to work for her in Milan. So in 1960, he returned home and worked for Krizia for three years. After some freelancing, he brought out his own line (produced by a brand called Mister Fox), where a love of precious fabrics and elegant Art Deco lines soon became his trademark.

"Each dress is a moment, a person, a place."
Walter Albini

Often seen with a gardenia in his jacket buttonhole, Albini has been credited with being the first ever "stylist" (as described by his friend, the journalist Anna Piaggi, 1931–2012). He is also referred to as the father of "prêt-à-porter", a concept he introduced in 1972, when he presented a collection in Milan's *Circolo del Giardino*. For this ambitious project, he designed for five different labels

WALTER ALBINI
PER
B A S I L E

As well as being a gifted fashion designer, Albini was a talented illustrator.
He graduated from the *Istituto d'Arte*, *Disegno e Moda* in Turin and moved
to Paris when he was 17, where he worked for newspapers and magazines.

(Callaghan, Basile, Escargot, Mister Fox and Diamant's), in
a show with over 100 models wearing affordable, beautiful
clothes. His objective? To make fashion accessible.

Albini was also instrumental in turning Milan into the
Italian fashion capital, away from Florence, when he created
Collezioni Donna, which eventually became the global
platform that is today Milan Fashion Week. A true creative
and pioneer, he died when he was just 42, leaving behind a
huge legacy that would shape the fashion industry forever.

Italian Icons

Above: A model wears an elegant hat, blouse and matching jacket
as part of Walter Albini's Autumn/Winter 1980 presentation.

Opposite: Albini's Autumn/Winter 1980 show displayed androgynous
silhouettes, perhaps inspired by the style of his friend, Coco Chanel.

¡SABELLA ROSSELL¡N¡

The charismatic Italian model, actress and filmmaker (b.1952) came from a legendary cinematic family – her father was the neorealist film director Roberto Rossellini and her mother was the Swedish screen siren, Ingrid Bergman. Known for her remarkable natural beauty (she has appeared on the cover of *Vogue* close to 30 times and on other pivotal fashion magazines), in 1982 she became the world's highest-paid model when she signed an exclusive deal with cosmetics giant Lancôme for her role as brand ambassador. The contract was terminated when she turned 43, but she re-joined 20 years later.

A talented actress, in 1986 she starred in David Lynch's cult movie *Blue Velvet*, a neo-noir thriller, with a stunning performance that compounded her acting career. She won an Independent Spirit Award for Best Female Lead in 1987; in addition, the film was nominated for Best Director at the Academy Awards and received an award for Best Film and Best Director from the National Society of Film Critics. She also appeared in the internationally acclaimed HBO TV movie *Crime of the Century* (1996), which received five Golden Globe nominations.

A fashion lover and style muse in her own right, photographed by such illustrious names as Richard Avedon and Helmut Newton, Rossellini also designed a line of bags for Bulgari (2010). A highlight of her illustrious modelling career was walking for Dolce & Gabbana (Spring/Summer 2019), wearing a tailored laced outfit. She was flanked by her son Roberto (wearing a silver suit with black detailing) and her daughter Elettra (with a multicoloured floral appliqué coat), gracefully carrying her eight-month-old son, Ronin. An Italian family affair – tradition at its best.

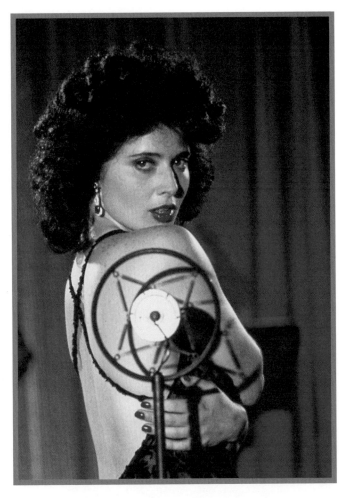

Above: Isabella Rossellini played singer Dorothy Vallens
in the American neo-noir mystery thriller *Blue Velvet*,
1986, written and directed by David Lynch.

Overleaf: Isabella Rossellini became the first face of Lancôme
in 1983, a role she fulfilled for over a decade.

Italian Icons

chapter 3

SETTIMANA DELLA MODA DI MILANO

Before the *Settimana della Moda di Milano* (MFW) was established, Italian fashion had been presented from 1951 onwards in Florence, when the entrepreneur Giovanni Battista Giorgini organized a runway show. It included designers such as Pucci and the Fontana sisters, and first took place in his own residence, Villa Torrigiani, where he invited an audience of buyers, photographers and international press. It was such a success that the next presentation took place at the halls of the Grand Hotel in Florence. Subsequent presentations were shown at the impressive Sala Bianca in the renaissance Palazzo Pitti building, a venue that still hosts regular fashion events such as *Pitti Uomo* (the men's ready-to-wear fashion trade fair) and is also home to The Costume Museum.

Roman catwalks had also become popular during the 1950s and '60s, due to the cinematic boom experienced at Cinecittà Film Studios and its string of celebrity Hollywood clients, but in 1958, major fashion events moved permanently to Milan and the city became known as one of the "Big Four" (alongside Paris, London and New York). Ever since, Milan has hosted this spectacular trade show twice a year, showcasing its forthcoming Autumn/Winter collections in February for womenswear and in January for men, and the Spring/Summer shows during September for women and

Designer Giorgio Armani seen here during a fitting in 2008.

Giorgio Armani's wardrobe for the 1980 movie *American Gigolo*, starring Richard Gere, embodied a new era in men's clothing, where textures and colour combinations broke away from the norm.

"Milan Fashion Week is where the glitz of the fashion season begins in earnest."

The *Washington Post*

in June for men. The events are partly organized by the *Camera Nazionale della Moda Italiana* (the National Chamber of Italian Fashion), which was founded that same year to promote and safeguard the industry.

During the 1970s Milan Fashion Week became the platform for many changes in fashion, such as the introduction of prêt-à-porter collections – a more accessible approach, away from couture, pioneered by Walter Albini. During the 1990s the term "supermodels" was coined on the Versace runway, logomania was born and, in contrast, Prada's minimalism was all the rage, turning fashion on its head.

Today, fashion week in this charming cobble-stoned city brings the age-old trade to life. Many events take place outdoors in some of its historic landmarks, such as the fifteenth-century Piazza Duomo (Milan's central square), the courtyard in fifteenth-century Castello Sforzesco and the Arco della Pace in Parco Sempione, which can be enjoyed by the general public. With some of the world's major fashion houses presenting their collections in Milan regularly (including Dolce & Gabbana, Gucci, Missoni, Prada, Versace and Armani), as well as emerging talent, this is a city that continues to inspire and where, it would seem, dreams do come true.

Here are some of our favourite MFW designers ...

Milan Fashion Week

GIORGIO ARMANI

Born in Piacenza in 1934 into a modest family, Giorgio Armani studied medicine at the University of Milan and later completed his two-year national military service before embarking on a fashion career at the age of 40. He started his creative journey at *La Rinascente* department store, where he was employed as a window dresser and was later promoted to the role of menswear buyer. Then, in 1964, he worked for Nino Cerruti and designed the *Cerruti Hitman* collection. After some freelance designing, he sold his Volkswagen Beetle to fund a new venture. With plenty of encouragement from his partner and business associate, the architect Sergio Galeotti ("Sergio made me believe in myself," he told *GQ* magazine in 2015), in 1975 he launched his own business: Giorgio Armani S.p.A.

From the offset, Armani's ready-to-wear collections reflected his trademark style: simplicity, elegance and a unique ability to effortlessly reinvent the classics, making them his own. One such example is the unstructured tailored jacket he introduced, with no lining or stiff padding, that could be worn by men and women, encapsulating his fresh, relaxed signature look. It lent itself to a glamorous clientele and resonated with a modern, more relatable idea of stardom. In 1978, for example, Diane Keaton wore an Armani ensemble with a tailored jacket when she received an Oscar for Best Actress for her performance in *Annie Hall* (1977) – the first in a long line of Armani red-carpet appearances.

Milan Fashion Week

An exquisite piece from the Autumn/Winter 2021 Giorgio Armani Privé Haute Couture collection, modelled by Cynthia Arrebola.

Giorgio Armani's Autumn/Winter 2022 Haute Couture
collection highlighted his skill and delicate craftsmanship
in a collection of stunning, feminine looks.

Armani's menswear has always been as strong as his women's
apparel and made its mark in 1980, when he dressed Richard
Gere for the US blockbuster *American Gigolo*, directed by
Paul Schrader (starring Richard Gere and Lauren Hutton).
The film displayed a stunning collection that showcased the
designer's use of texture and contrasting colours as well as
the impeccable clean lines of his tailoring, placing him firmly
on the fashion map. Here, broader shoulders and wide lapels
reflected the power-dressing image of the eighties economic
boom, creating a strong silhouette that captured the

essence of this time. He has since outfitted over 200 movies including Brian De Palma's *The Untouchables* in 1987 with Kevin Costner and Robert De Niro and Martin Scorsese's *The Wolf of Wall Street* in 2013 (starring Leonardo DiCaprio as a ruthless Wall Street trader) and dressed Jodie Foster, a close friend and one of his favourite actresses, in the science-fiction movie *Elysium*, by Neill Blomkamp, also in 2013.

Since its inception, the Armani brand has undergone a huge expansion, with several lines being introduced over time, catering for different sectors of the market. In 1979, two successful children's lines, Armani Junior and Armani Baby, were launched (with the first Armani Junior exclusive store opening in Milan in 1986). Three years later, in 1981, a casual label called Armani Jeans was created, with a focus on off-duty clothing and athleisure. Another diffusion line, Armani Collezione, followed in 1982, based on the main Armani line but sold at a more accessible lower-price point.

Perfume was also introduced in 1988, when the company licensed L'Oréal as their cosmetics partner and later added beauty products and make-up to their offerings. Armani Casa was another diffusion line selling high-end furniture, textiles and home décor, which was set up in 2000, adding a lifestyle dimension to the brand. And in 2005, Armani also launched its first made-to-measure haute couture line, Armani Privé, which, alongside Giorgio Armani and Emporio Armani, shows seasonal collections at Milan Fashion Week.

Mr Armani, as he is known in the industry, has not only enriched Italian fashion by creating simple luxury and elegant fantasy, but has set the bar high and inspired many by envisioning an aspirational image based on his aesthetic. You can enjoy the Armani experience by dining in one of their many restaurants and even stay in one of their luxe hotels in Dubai and Milan to enjoy every last detail.

BENETTON

In 1955, when Luciano Benetton was just 20 years old and selling newspapers in his home town of Treviso, he had a brilliant idea: to add colour to people's clothes because he wanted "to make them happier". At the time, his sister was selling home-made knitted sweaters, so he invested in a knitting machine and plenty of bright yarns so that she could produce them faster, and together, they sold them to local shops. With the help of his siblings, Giuliana (as head of design), Carlo (in charge of production) and Gilberto (admin director), by 1965 the Benetton brand was born. A store was opened in Belluno (1965), one in Paris (1969) and another on New York's Madison Avenue (1980).

With a preppie aesthetic and a focus on quality, Benetton became hugely popular during the 1980s and '90s, and was a big hit with youth sub-cultures such as the "Milanese Paninaro", a smart/casual aspirational clan with a passion for cool brands and logos, who would wear rugby shirts, denim and Moncler puffer jackets, while hanging out with their friends in town (originally at the Al Panino, hence the name, as well as in fast-food restaurant chains like McDonald's).

Aside from its classic, quality clothing, which was as comfortable as it was colourful, Benetton became known for its unconventional marketing strategies, which delivered

Opposite: Benetton's Spring/Summer 2020 show was a colourful, playful presentation.

Overleaf: Highlighting diversity, a group of models wear looks from the United Colors of Benetton's Spring/Summer 2023 global collection, which took place in Mumbai.

Milan Fashion Week

political and social messages, creating thought-provoking and controversial advertising campaigns that obtained huge audiences at a pre-social media time. In 1982, the art director and photographer Oliviero Toscani joined the company and was in charge of many of its legendary campaigns. Ahead of his time, in 1984 he shot the United Colours of Benetton campaign, which featured models from several different ethnic backgrounds. He also created a series of polemic lifestyle photography ads, including a picture of a newborn baby with its umbilical cord still intact, a nun kissing a priest and the "Unhate" campaign (2011), which showed world political and faith leaders kissing – including the then US President Obama kissing Venezuela's President, Hugo Chávez. As stated by Alessandro Benetton, Luciano's son and executive deputy chairman of the Benetton Group at the time:

"[The campaign] fits perfectly with the values and history of Benetton, which chooses social issues and actively promotes humanitarian causes that could not otherwise have been communicated on a global scale."

In 1974, Benetton introduced Sisley (a more formal collection) and Playlife (everyday clothing) to their portfolio. This was followed by their award-winning magazine *COLOURS* (1991–2014), edited by Oliviero Toscani and art director Tibor Kalman, which promoted a message of diversity. It was hugely influential in the graphic design world, becoming a platform for new talent.

Another Benetton enterprise, away from the fashion scene, has been their involvement in Formula 1. During the 1980s they sponsored Tyrell, the English team, and later, Italy's Alfa Romeo. But in 1986, Luciano made the bold move of taking over an entire team, paying approximately £2 million (US $2,526,000) for it. The team achieved a handful of victories between 1988 and 1990; and in 1991 they signed the German

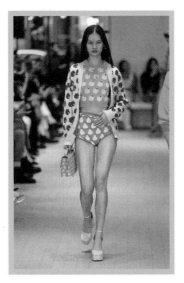

Contrasting colourways are mismatched at Benetton's Spring/Summer 2023 show, the first presentation under the newly appointed creative designer, Andrea Incontri.

racing driver Michael Schumacher, who went on to win two Grand Prix championship titles under Team Benetton. Eventually, Benetton sold the Italian Formula 1 team to Renault, but their love of sport remains active through *La Ghirada*, a sports complex built in 1982, near Treviso, that extends over 22 hectares (220,000 m²), with basketball, golf, volleyball, rugby and water sports facilities. The brand is also patron of Volley Treviso, Treviso's own volleyball team.

Benetton's diverse, rainbow approach to life, from the first hand-knitted sweaters they made to the latest collections on offer, is as relevant today as it ever was; and with a strong, adventurous spirit, it remains the go-to brand for casual chic Italian fashion.

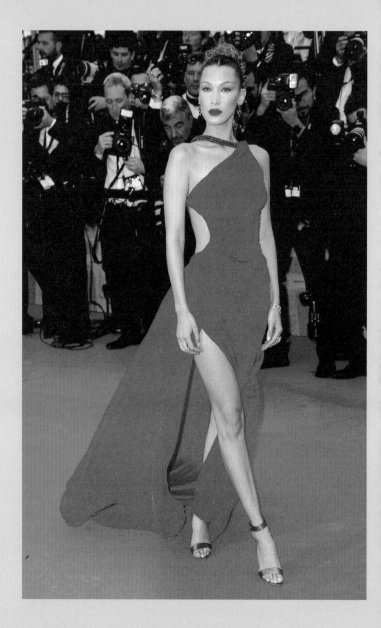

ROBERTO CAVALLI

Cavalli, the exquisite Italian fashion house, is best known for taking a walk on the wild side. Exotic skins and opulence are defining traits of its highly decorative and flamboyant aesthetic, which has enjoyed a recent revival with the vintage trend of the nineties and noughties.

Born in Florence on November 15, 1940, Roberto Cavalli studied at his local Art Institute, with a focus on textiles. His grandfather, the artist Giuseppe Rossi (a member of the Macchiaioli movement) exhibited his work in Florence's illustrious Uffizi Gallery. Roberto no doubt inherited his talent; while still a student, a number of his designs attracted interest from some of the major Italian hosiery factories.

Always innovative, during the 1970s Cavalli developed and patented a ground-breaking printing technique on leather that created a patchwork effect, something that Hermès and Pierre Cardin commissioned from him *tout suite*. In 1972 he showed his work for the first time in Paris, later on the catwalk of the *Sala Bianca* at the Pitti Palace in Florence and eventually in Milan. In 1972 he also opened his first store, in the fittingly glamorous Saint-Tropez. This was his time to shine, with jet-set customers that included Sophia Loren and Brigitte Bardot, whose sensuous, effortless elegance embodied the spirit of his collections.

Opposite: An eye-catching red Roberto Cavalli dress is worn by Bella Hadid at the *Pain and Glory* premiere, 2019, held at the *Grand Théâtre Lumière* during the 72nd Cannes Film Festival.

Overleaf: Glamour and animal prints are characteristic of Roberto Cavalli's style, as seen at the Spring/Summer 2022 fashion show.

Milan Fashion Week

In 1994 he presented his iconic sand-blasted denim collection in Milan for the first time – a distressed look that appealed to a younger audience – and later that year he opened boutiques in Saint Barth (in the French Caribbean), as well as in Venice and Saint-Tropez. The minimal fashion that became prominent during the nineties, however, wasn't a trend he subscribed to. "That was the beginning of Japanese fashion; everything went minimal," he told the *Evening Standard* at the time. "Black and white. You understand it was not my time." But that didn't stop his unique, feminine style from shining bright, making the brand an all-time bestseller with an ever-growing portfolio.

His lines include the luxurious and sophisticated Roberto Cavalli Women (launched in 1970), Just Cavalli (an urban take on the brand founded in 1998), Cavalli Class (a premium diffusion line launched in 1998), Roberto Cavalli Men (1990), Roberto Cavalli Eyewear (1999) and Roberto Cavalli Junior (2000). The company continued to expand, and in 2002 Cavalli opened a boutique with a café in the centre of Florence, shortly followed by one in Milan called Just Cavalli Café in Torre Branca, as well as a boutique on the legendary Via della Spiga. Then, in 2005, he was asked to update the *Playboy* Bunny outfit, ready for the launch of the Playboy Tower, which he did by raising the leg line and streamlining the overall costume.

Roberto Cavalli Fragrances followed (2011), as well as Roberto Cavalli Home (2012), RC Sport (2012), Roberto Cavalli Watches and RC Haute Couture (2013) – sold online and in over 50 countries worldwide.

Bohemian patchwork references with a seventies influence were key in the Spring/Summer 2017 Roberto Cavalli show.

"I copy the dress of an animal because I love to copy God. I think God is the most fantastic designer."

Roberto Cavalli

Creative directors at the company's helm have included Peter Dundas in 2015 and Paul Surridge (2017). Following financial difficulties, in 2015 a ninety per cent share of the business was sold to investor Clessidra Private Equity SGR, which in turn was bought by Dubai-based Vision Investment Group LLC in 2019. The appointment of Fausto Puglisi in 2021 as creative consultant, however, was instrumental to the brand's repositioning in Milan's prestigious fashion scene.

Once nicknamed "King of Bling", Cavalli remains a favourite on the red carpet, from Hollywood to Cannes, dressing celebrities such as Jennifer Lopez, the Beckhams and Lady Gaga. His exquisite tailoring and timeless elegance has secured him a place in the Italian fashion industry as we enjoy his collections on the Milanese runway season after season.

Roberto Cavalli's Spring/Summer 2017 presentation was designed by Peter Dundas, who referenced American textiles such as Navajo blankets.

DOLCE & GABBANA

Domenico Dolce (b.1958) and Stefano Gabbana (b.1962) were both working for designer Giorgio Correggiari in the early 1980s, but actually met in a nightclub in Milan in 1982. They went on to set up their own consulting studio in 1983 and presented their first women's collection in 1985. Also abbreviated to D&G, the luxury fashion house began on a very tight budget: unable to hire professionals, they asked their friends to model and to use their own accessories in the show – a sheet from Domenico's home was even used as a curtain on the stage.

Despite low sales and early financial challenges, the pair quickly became hugely influential in the Italian fashion scene – thanks to their sophisticated aesthetic, attention to detail and commitment to quality. They would become best known for their intricate prints (mostly florals, fruits and animal-inspired designs), embroidery and black lace – often seen juxtaposed. Their main source of inspiration has always been their homeland in its many guises – strong Italian neorealist film imagery, Catholic symbols (such as rosaries or crosses) and colourful Mediterranean scenes.

Their fourth collection, launched in the late eighties, was particularly well received by the press, who coined the term *The Sicilian Dress* to describe one of their pieces after it got a mention in Hal Rubenstein's book, *100 Unforgettable Dresses* (2011), making fashion history. Its construction was based on classic underwear, with straps, creating a distinctive feminine shape. As described by Rubenstein, "The Sicilian dress is the essence of Dolce & Gabbana, the brand's sartorial touchstone." This was also the start of lingerie dressing, a trend where underwear became outerwear. Their beautifully

The Dolce & Gabbana Ready-to-Wear Spring/Summer 2022 fashion show featured plenty of timeless garments, including this figure-hugging black dress.

Dolce & Gabbana's Spring/Summer 2018 show was called "Queen of Hearts" and took many guises. This yellow floor-length dress with a print featuring vegetables was worn with matching carrot earrings.

assembled and flattering black bra, in particular, is a symbol of this tendency, appearing repeatedly in their collections in endless iterations.

Following the success of their womenswear, the brand developed a menswear line in 1990, a category for which, a year later, they received the Woolmark Award for the most innovative collection. A line of accessories (including shoes) and cosmetics was later added to their conglomerate and in 1991 they made the international headlines when Madonna wore a Dolce & Gabbana jacket and corset with coloured, encrusted gemstones to the New York City premiere of the documentary *Truth or Dare: In Bed with Madonna* (1991). They also designed the singer's costumes for her Drowned World Tour (2001) and for many other performers on stage, such as Missy Elliott, Beyoncé, Whitney Houston and Kylie Minogue.

Following this momentum, a new line was created in 1994, directed to a younger demographic, which they called "D&G". Later, in 2012, they launched the Alta Moda line, an haute couture collection that not only embraced Italian heritage and craftmanship but has continued to push the boundaries, creating confident, sensual and provocative ensembles inspired by Sicilian culture while paying tribute to their rich heritage. The year 2012 was also the year they integrated D&G into their main collection in an attempt to consolidate and strengthen the brand.

Dolce & Gabbana have also been known for their distinctive advertising campaigns, which are invariably beautifully styled, if sometimes controversial. Often shot in black and white, they sometimes portray cross-generational family scenes and close-up portraits (Autumn/Winter 2012, Autumn/Winter 2015), busy group shots taken outdoors, celebrating life in the bright sunshine (Spring/Summer 2016, Spring/Summer 2018) and, especially in their perfume images, sensual or romantic photographs set in arresting coastlines (for example, the Light Blue perfume advertising campaign, 2010). They offer a snapshot of an idyllic lifestyle that is a unique blend of glamour, romantic luxury and a touch of bohemian nostalgia.

For their Spring/Summer 2023 show, Kim Kardashian acted as muse for the collection and face of the brand, drawing inspiration from her very own archive of D&G pieces. Photography duo Mert & Marcus (Mert Alaş and Marcus Piggott) shot the stunning black and white campaign.

Above: Religious motifs, so characteristic of the brand, were seen on clothing and accessories at Dolce & Gabbana's Spring/Summer 2017 catwalk show.

Opposite: Dolce & Gabbana's Spring/Summer 2017 collection was a fresh interpretation of their signature style, with baroque-embellished T-shirts and beaded shorts.

The renowned Italian fashion house Etro was founded in 1968 by Gerolamo Etro (known to his friends as "Gimmo") as a textile company. He was a cultured man with a love of the arts, whose intention was to create beautiful fabrics for the emerging fashion industry – something his wife Roberta, an antique dealer who owned an exquisite collection of shawls and cashmere gowns, fully appreciated.

A turning point in their story was the introduction of a paisley print in 1981 which, over time, became synonymous with the brand in its many versions and colour combinations. The print was as emblematic as it was versatile and welcomed by all – from members of the upper echelons of society to rock stars like Mick Jagger. So much so that a rich archive of paisley textiles and art is kept in the in-house library at the headquarters in the Etro building, on Milan's Via Spartaco. Another distinctive feature of the Etro brand is their logo. It depicts a Pegasus, an elegant leaping horse with wings, representing the spirit of adventure, freedom and timelessness that Etro stands for. The logo is often seen embroidered or embossed on garments and accessories.

During the eighties, the brand grew into different markets: in 1983 the company opened their first flagship Milanese store on Via Bigli, offering ties, scarves and shawls, and in 1984, it started to produce leather goods. The following year, a home collection was launched (first with home textiles and pillows and later with ceramics, gifts and wallpaper), and fragrances followed in 1989.

When at the helm, Gimmo would take his four children to the office on Saturdays and eventually, one by one, they all

Fluid shapes and earthy tones were present at the
Etro Spring/Summer 2010 collection.

Above: Etro Menswear Spring/Summer 2015 was a strong collection with plenty of colour-blocking and powerful prints.

Overleaf: For Etro's Menswear Spring/Summer 2023, Kean and Veronica Etro presented a bohemian collection that was inspired by poetry. Instead of traditional invites, the guests received a phone call from an actor reciting a poem to them.

joined the family business – although they had to start at the bottom. Ippolito Etro recalls his father telling him, "If you work here, you have to start from scratch." And so they did, each bringing to the table a very different skillset but united in their love for the family brand. Jacopo Etro began working for the company in 1982 and was creative director of the Etro Accessories, Leather, Home and Textile collections, as well as working as head of communications. Kean Etro became creative director of Etro Man from 1990, sourcing inspiration from his travels, having joined as a digital intern in 1986. Ippolito Etro started in 1991, working in the administration department before he became general director; and Veronica, the youngest sibling, joined the firm after graduating from London's Central Saint Martins in 1997, and in 2000 became creative director for their women's collections. From 2017 onwards, Veronica and Kean began showing their collections together.

Etro's first fashion show at Milan Fashion Week took place in 1996 and became a permanent fixture there, eagerly awaited season after season by fashion editors and stylists alike. A shake-up in the business structure took place in 2022 when Marco de Vincenzo, the first designer to join from outside the family, was appointed the new creative director for the women's, men's and home collections.

This lifestyle brand has been at the heart of the "Made in Italy" movement since its inception, with complete commitment to craftsmanship and top-quality fabrics such as silk, cashmere and cotton in extraordinary colour combinations. "Etro style" has, in fact, been described as "art applied to prêt-à-porter" at Etro.com: a journey of exploration where lovingly curated garments tell the story of one of Italy's most successful luxury family businesses – a business that is always "faithful to beauty," according to Ippolito Etro.

FENDi

In 1925, a talented designer named Adele Casagrande and her visionary husband, Edoardo Fendi, opened a leather and fur shop on Rome's Via del Plebiscito. The shop, known as Fendi, soon became famous for its exquisite craftsmanship and before too long, in 1932, the couple were opening a larger store on the popular Via Piave. The Fendis had five daughters, Paola, Franca, Alda, Anna and Carla – all of whom went into the family business. The new generation was now in charge and their different strengths and unstoppable energy transformed the business into one of Italy's most important fashion houses of all time. With a booming economy behind them, in 1964 the sisters opened a larger store on the Via de la Borgognona – frequented by Italian movie stars Sophia Loren and Claudia Cardinale – and in 1965 hired the German designer Karl Lagerfeld as creative director of fur, a partnership referred to by Silvia Venturini Fendi as "fashion's greatest love story", which was to last 54 years until Lagerfeld's death in 2019. One of the first things Lagerfeld did was to redesign their logo and create the legendary "double F", which stood for "fun furs". Ground-breaking techniques were created and boundaries were challenged, marking the start of a new era.

Some of the most emblematic fashion shows in history have been staged by Fendi. For Spring/Summer 2008, an impressive collection was presented at the Great Wall of China, in front of 500 exclusive guests, who were mesmerized by the beautiful collection on 88 models (the number eight representing good luck in Chinese culture) walking along the 88-metre (288.714 ft) runway at sunset. And to celebrate their ninetieth anniversary in 2016, the second Haute Fourrure (high fur) collection, "Legends and Fairy Tales", took place

Above: Kim Jones's Autumn/Winter 2023 collection included some knits inspired by the Autumn/Winter 1996 collection that Karl Lagerfeld had designed for the House of Fendi.

Overleaf: Bella Hadid opened Fendi's Autumn/Winter 2022 collection wearing a delicate sheer dress and pale green accessories.

Vittoria Ceretti walks the catwalk for Fendi's Spring/Summer 2022 collection, wearing a striking belted, multicoloured fur coat.

at Rome's Trevi Fountain, after a great deal of restoration work to which Fendi donated €2.6 million ($2,758). With a glass platform covering the water, the models looked magical, as if floating in their stunning couture, in a collection that displayed extraordinary techniques, including fur intarsia and printed mink, silk and organza.

In 1992, Anna's daughter, Silvia Venturini Fendi, was appointed artistic director of Accessories and Menswear and in 1997, she created one of the most famous handbags in history: the Fendi "Baguette". "I was asked to come up with a particularly easy and functional handbag," she explained to *Style.com*. "It had to be technological and minimal, just like the times. My response was the 'Baguette' – the exact opposite of what was requested of me." The design rose to international fame when featured on the arm of Sarah Jessica Parker playing Carrie Bradshaw in HBO's blockbuster, *Sex and The City* (1998–2004). To celebrate its 25th anniversary, a very special fashion show, Fendi's Resort 2023 runway collection, was staged in New York's Manhattan Hammerstein Ballroom, with collaborations from Sarah Jessica Parker, Marc Jacobs and Tiffany and Co.

Following Lagerfeld's death in 2019, British designer Kim Jones was appointed Womenswear artistic director, marking the start of an exciting, brand-new chapter for the House. With a fresh approach, his debut was the Spring/Summer 2021 Couture collection, which he called the "journey from Bloomsbury to Borghese". Based on Virginia Woolf's 1928 novel *Orlando*, the lavish show was a family affair, with Silvia Venturini Fendi designing some of the accessories, including some mother-of-pearl minaudières, and Delfina Delettrez, Silvia's daughter (now appointed Fendi's artistic director of Jewellery) adding her expertise. A stellar cast included actress Demi Moore, model Kate Moss (Accessories consultant for the presentation) and her daughter, Lila Grace Moss Hack; Christy Turlington and her nephew, James Turlington; Adwoa Aboah and her sister, Kesewa Aboah, and Leonetta Fendi and Delfina Delettrez (Silvia's daughters).

Honouring Fendi's legacy, Jones's collections combine artisanal craftsmanship with modern concepts and, above all, a sense of beauty, tradition and quintessential Italian savoir faire. And with Silvia Venturini Fendi and Delfina Delettrez at the heart of the design team (despite LVMH's majority stake acquisition in 2001), the House of Fendi is still very much a family affair.

Milan Fashion Week

Above: Actress Sarah Jessica Parker attends Fendi's "25th Anniversary of the Baguette" show in 2022, at the Hammerstein Ballroom in New York City, holding a Baguette she designed as part of a limited-edition capsule collection.

Opposite: Fendi's Spring/Summer 2022 was a contemporary collection with a disco feel to it, influenced by the work of illustrator Antonio Lopez, who had been a friend of Karl Lagerfeld.

SALVATORE FERRAGAMO

Salvatore Ferragamo (1898–1960), the eleventh of fourteen children, grew up in Bonito, a village close to Naples. His extraordinary story begins when, at the age of nine, he handcrafted a pair of white shoes (working overnight with borrowed materials) for his sister Giuseppina's first communion, because his family couldn't afford to buy her a pair. Despite his father's career choice disapproval – he dismissed shoemaking as being too basic a profession – at just eleven years of age, Salvatore decided to move to Naples, where he learned the trade from the best craftsmen in the business. Back in his hometown, he opened a shoe shop in his parents' house which, driven by his passion and innovation, became hugely successful: he had found his calling in life.

Salvatore was just sixteen when he decided to join some of his brothers, who had emigrated to the United States, getting a job at Boston's Plant Shoe Factory. But only two weeks later he decided that the machine processes used there were interfering with the end result. So he moved to Santa Barbara in California in 1915 and instead opened a repair shop, where he also created made-to-measure footwear. He also joined the University of Southern California to study anatomy, chemical engineering and maths to ensure his creations were as comfortable as they were attractive.

His timing couldn't have been better: the first American cinema studios were emerging and all their actors required beautiful shoes. He followed the industry to Hollywood and, in 1923, opened the Hollywood Boot Shop, making shoes for

During the 1950s Salvatore Ferragamo designed footwear for royalty and for many movie stars from Hollywood's golden era.

actresses like Greta Garbo and Gloria Swanson, and became known among the press as the "Shoemaker to the Stars".

Ferragamo moved back to Florence in 1927. A visionary, he had developed new techniques that were met with resistance from local masters, so he opened his own factory, where he trained 75 apprentices to create shoes which would be exported to the US. The Wall Street Crash two years later affected his business significantly, but he was able to continue working and rented some space in the medieval Palazzo Spini Feroni in Florence, which he was eventually able to buy, and which was to become his permanent HQ.

During the First World War, some of the essential materials he utilized had become scarce, but Ferragamo transformed these challenges into opportunities by using hemp, felt, needlepoint, lace, cellophane, raffia and cork (his cork wedges were patented in 1937) and even experimented with fish skins as possible replacements.

Aside from the acclaimed wedges he designed in 1937 and 1938 (such as the platform "Rainbow Sandal" originally created for Judy Garland, who loved wearing heels), some of his most famous designs include the invisible sandals (using nylon fishing line, 1947) with a wooden base, his "caged" heels and the "Viatica" four-inch heel pumps – Marilyn Monroe's favourite "Ferragamos" (featured in *Some Like it Hot*, 1959). The designer also patented a heel created especially for Monroe, made of steel and wood to provide maximum comfort, creating – according to some – the first pair of stilettos, named after a pointed, slim Italian dagger.

By the 1950s, Ferragamo was so much in demand that he was employing 700 craftsmen and making over 340 pairs of shoes every day. Orders were divided into three customer categories: "Cinderella" shoes (smaller than a size six, with customers including Joan Crawford, whom he described as "fashion lovers who needed to be in love to be happy"), "Venuses" (size six, like Marilyn Monroe, who were beautiful but loved the simple things in life – something which often confused people); and the "Aristocrats", who wore a size seven and beyond (who, like Audrey Hepburn, were – according to his classification – sensitive, understanding and sometimes moody).

Maximilian Davis's debut show for Ferragamo, Spring/Summer 2023, had plenty of tailoring and colourful fabrics. As part of their rebranding, the brand has now dropped "Salvatore" from its name.

"Give a girl the right pair of shoes and she can conquer the world."

Marilyn Monroe

Salvatore Ferragamo died in 1960, at the age of 62. His wife Wanda took over the company, together with their two eldest daughters, Fiamma (who created the "Vara" pumps, a rounded shoe with a low block heel and a grosgrain bow, introduced in 1978) and Giovanna who created the first ready-to-wear collection for the house in 1967. The family business grew from couture footwear to accessories (including eyewear, bags and watches), perfumes and ready-to-wear collections. British designer Maximilian Davis has been their creative director since 2022.

A museum celebrating Salvatore Ferragamo's extraordinary legacy, and the brilliant mind that pushed so many boundaries, opened in Florence in 1995 at the Palazzo Spini Feroni, where he had once based his atelier. It holds over 10,000 shoes, including some key pieces from his footwear collections, and a handbag collection.

A stunning wheel of colour made of Ferragamo shoes was created for the exhibition "Salvatore Ferragamo Evolving Legend 1928–2008" at the Museum of Contemporary Art in Shanghai, China.

American television presenter and singer Ashley Roberts is spotted wearing a colourful Fiorucci ensemble in central London, 2020.

FiORUCCi

Founded in 1967 by Milanese designer Elio Fiorucci (1935–2015), this is a brand that captured the spirit of the time as well as its youth culture. The son of a shoemaker, Elio started to work in his father's store when he was fourteen, and in 1962 designed a successful brightly-coloured waterproof overshoe that was featured in *Amica* magazine. He went travelling with his earnings, spending time in London, a scene which was bursting with fashion trends, and came back with boundless inspiration and ideas.

Fiorucci is known for creating stretched denim with Lycra (in 1982, he made the very first stretched jeans, using the fabric invented by DuPont), for its vinyl trousers, for using bright and fluorescent colours, as well as for its provocative and rebellious imagery. The iconic logo, featuring two angels wearing sunglasses, made its appearance in 1971 and was seen on many of their items, famously on the legendary graphic T-shirts.

Elio Fiorucci also transformed the retail experience by creating the blueprint of a global concept store that went beyond simply purchasing fashion. It was a carefully curated space with eclectic fashion, unique beauty items, music (including DJ decks ready to mix the latest disco hits) and home furnishings, predating today's immersive lifestyle shopping experience. The first Fiorucci destination store, inspired by London's Carnaby Street and its vibrant youth culture, opened in Milan in 1967 and became known as Day-Glo Heaven. More followed: another Milanese shop opened in 1974 (this one also had a fast-food restaurant), a boutique was launched on London's King's Road in 1975 and the famous store on New York's East 59th Street, referred to as the

Milan Fashion Week

"Went to Fiorucci and it's so much fun there. It's everything I've always wanted, all plastic."

Andy Warhol (December 21, 1983 diary entry)

"daytime Studio 54", opened in 1976, offering music and free espresso to all its customers. It became an institution, the place to be (a young Marc Jacobs skipped summer school to frequent the store), acquiring a cult following and a creative community whose regulars included Madonna, Jackie O, Cher and Andy Warhol (who became friends with Elio and chose the location for the launch of his mythical magazine, *Interview*). Another notable collaboration took place with pop artist Keith Haring and Angel Ortiz (the graffiti artist known as LA II), who in 1983 were invited to paint the Milan store. It was a site performance that took them 13 hours overnight to complete, painting 5,000 square feet (465 square meters) to the tunes of DJ Maurizio Marisco.

In 1990, Fiorucci sold the brand to the Japanese company, Edwin Co. Ltd. And, in 2003, he founded Love Therapy as a continuation of his romantic vision – he would often say, "Love will save the world."

Fiorucci was acquired in 2015 by the British businesswoman Janie Schaffer (founder of Knickerbox) and her business partner and former husband, Stephen Schaffer. Two years later, Fiorucci was relaunched, unveiling a new destination store in the heart of London's Soho, 50 years after the very first store was opened in Milan. In 2022, it was bought by the Swiss investor Dona Bertarelli, with Alessandro Pisani as CEO and Francesca Murri as the new creative director.

With previous experience at Versace, Giorgio Armani, Gucci, Givenchy and Ferragamo, Murri brought the brand to Milan Fashion Week

With such a distinctive visual identity and unstoppable energy, this extraordinary brand soon became part of popular culture. It transformed streetwear by bringing some fun into the "Made in Italy" movement and faithfully represented youth culture worldwide. Giorgio Armani, who once described Elio Fiorucci as a revolutionary, said, "He was always ready to take some risks to really understand his time." Fiorucci leaves a legacy of rock, pop and creativity, as well as some classic looks with plenty of attitude.

British singer and songwriter Rod Stewart is photographed wearing a Fiorucci vest, c.1975.

In 1921, Guccio Gucci (1881–1953) founded the celebrated luxury empire House of Gucci. Born into a family of leather goods artisans in Florence, Guccio moved to London in 1897, where he worked as a porter in The Savoy hotel. While there, he was inspired by the beautifully built luggage the customers travelled with and on his return to Florence in 1902, he got a job at the Valigeria Franzi, an established Milanese manufacturer of leather bags and luggage, where he dreamed of starting his own business. In time he became a master of his trade (the 178 components of a Franzi handbag take over 12 hours to handcraft) and by 1921, he was ready to open his first store on Florence's Via della Vigna Nuova, where he sold luggage and handmade saddles of the finest materials.

After the Second World War, as material shortages – leather in particular – posed a challenge, the Gucci artisans began working with bamboo, which was lightweight and durable. This led to their successful Gucci "Bamboo" bag in 1947, a saddle-shaped handbag which became an icon of its time, as carried by Elizabeth Taylor and Princess Grace Kelly of Monaco. The interlocking GG logo, which is still used today, was designed in 1933.

The 1950s were a fruitful decade for the brand, now with a global tagline that read "Quality is remembered long after

Opposite: Designed by Alessandro Michele, Gucci's Spring/Summer 2022 Love Parade show took place in Hollywood, California.

Overleaf: Gucci's men's Spring/Summer 2016 eccentric collection was described by Vogue.com as "the New Punk".

Milan Fashion Week

price is forgotten". In 1951, the brand's red and green stripe was introduced and the first Gucci store was opened in Milan, on the Via Monte Napoleone. Two years later, Gucci broke the US market, opening a store in the Savoy Plaza Hotel, on East 58th Street, New York. This was a very symbolic move for the House, representative of Guccio's time working as a bellboy and dreaming of building his own brand.

Sadly, Guccio died shortly after the New York opening. Upon his death, the shares of his company were distributed between his three sons, Aldo, Vasco and Rodolfo, leaving the management of the brand now fully in their charge. Aldo was responsible for the US operations, Vasco managed business in Florence and Rodolfo looked after Milan. Classics were designed, including the famed Gucci "Horsebit Loafer" (1953) and the "Horsebit" bag (1955). Such was their success that a store opened in Paris in 1963. Another much-admired piece, the "Flora" scarf (a print commissioned by the established

The double-G Gucci logo has stood the test of time and is still as relevant today as it was when a stylized version of the original 1923 design was created by Aldo Gucci, Guccio's son, in 1933.

Italian artist Vittorio Accornero) was designed for Princess
Grace Kelly of Monaco in 1966.

The 1980s were dominated by a series of family feuds which
started between Guccio's sons and were carried into the
next generation. When Rodolfo died in 1983, he left his
son Maurizio a majority stake in the company. Aldo and
Maurizio had very different visions for the House, which led
to a string of lawsuits and legal battles that ended in 1993,
when Maurizio was forced to sell his fifty per cent share to
investors. Gucci then ceased to be a family business.

Under new management, in 1994 a Texan designer was hired
as creative director to oversee the Women's collections,
an appointment that would shape the brand's trajectory in
unimaginable ways. Enter Tom Ford. His vision for Gucci
was revolutionary, leaving behind its traditional image,
which had become outdated, and embracing a much simpler,
minimalist and sexy aesthetic that defined the decade. His
Autumn/Winter 1995 collection was a turning point, featuring
sensual unbuttoned silk shirts and velvet suits and trousers,
and the show he presented in Autumn/Winter 1996 was
smooth and streamlined, with sexy white cut-out dresses. In
addition to his incredible talent as a designer, off the runway
he masterminded a very effective and provocative – even
scandalous – advertising campaign style, in collaboration
with Carine Roitfeld (who worked as his stylist) and
photographer Mario Testino.

In 2004, Tom Ford left Gucci, which was owned by the luxury
fashion conglomerate PPR (now Kering) and went on to
pursue his very successful eponymous label, a decision that, as
he told *Women's Wear Daily* at the time, "was about control".

Frida Giannini, who had worked as handbag design director
at Gucci since 2002, became creative director of the women's

A striking striped ensemble was seen in Gucci's Cruise 2023 collection, which took place at the thirteenth-century Castel del Monte, located in the Apulia region of Italy.

prêt-à-porter collections and accessories in 2005 and was appointed creative director of the House in 2006. Her tenure took Gucci into a new direction that was feminine and sensual, with a bohemian edge. She also focused on accessories and drew on the brand's popular handbags (the bamboo design from 1947 and the "Constance" style designed in 1961, renamed "Jackie" after Jackie O because it was a favourite of hers), releasing new versions of them. Frida left Gucci in 2014 (along with Gucci's CEO, Patrizio di Marco). She was set to depart at the end of February (after showing her Autumn/Winter 2015 menswear collection), but she left suddenly and her collection was substituted five days before the presentation. Her own work was never shown.

Alessandro Michele replaced Giannini, which was a surprise to many, including himself. "I wasn't even on the list," he told *Vogue* magazine. Michele had started working at Gucci in 2002 and was in charge of the handbag designs. His first show (menswear Autumn/Winter 2015) was created in under a week and expressed a completely new vision for the brand: androgynous shapes, flowing silhouettes, pussy-bow shirts and sandals with a maximalist twist. This was a look he extended into the womenswear too, championing an intellectual, all-inclusive and "more is more" aesthetic, away from the sexy, slick jet-set image Gucci had become known for. In 2022, after twenty years at the company (seven as creative director), Michele left Gucci, who were looking for a fresh direction that would push sales further. He was replaced by Sabato De Sarno, who joined from Valentino and initiated a new era for the House.

Despite its chequered history, the essence of the House of Gucci remains undiluted. Celebrating Guccio's original vision, the label has become known for being beautifully created in Italy by masters of their craft and for redefining luxury. Gucci stands for sophisticated elegance.

MiSSOHi

Ottavio Missoni, known to his close friends and family as "Tai", was an established athlete (competing in the 400-metre run category and then in the 400-metre hurdles) before becoming a fashion designer. A member of the Italian National Team, he represented his country at the Summer Olympic Games in London in 1948. With the help of his teammate Giorgio Oberweger, he made a collection of knitted training tracksuits, called Venjulia suits, which became the team's uniform. It was also in London where he met his future wife, Rosita Jelmini, whom he married in 1953.

Colour has always been at the heart of Missoni, as seen in this early multicoloured striped outfit, complete with a matching bonnet.

The couple set up a knitting workshop in Gallarate, Northern Italy, and in 1958 presented their first collection, called "Milano Sympathy", which became known for its colourful geometric designs at Milan's La Rinascente department store. During the 1960s, their clothes began to appear in fashion magazines and, as their popularity grew, they moved to bigger premises, where they experimented with new fabrics such as viscose and rayon, blending them together. In 1965, Italian journalist Anna Piaggi, who was working as fashion editor for *Arianna* magazine, became a fan of the brand and a friend of the family, her support being instrumental to the brand's expansion.

Rosita then went to New York, where she met Emmanuelle Khanh, with whom Missoni collaborated the following season, in 1967. As the brand expanded, they were invited to show at the Pitti Palace in Florence. Backstage, as she was helping the models prepare, Rosita asked them to take off their bras to ensure the straps didn't show under the dresses. Under the bright lights, however, the clothes became see-through and Missoni were not invited to the next season. But, with no such thing as bad publicity, they started to sell in Paris, having secured their first magazine cover in *Arianna* magazine (1967) and then one in French *Elle* (1968). Soon they were featured in *Women's Wear Daily* in the US (1969) and met Diana Vreeland (US *Vogue*'s editor-in-chief at the time), who organized meetings with buyers that would lead to the first Missoni boutique opening in New York's Bloomingdale's department store in 1970.

Missoni clothes have always been beautifully made, using only the best materials – from silk jersey to viscose and exquisite knits in colourful patterns. Such is their quality, many are available in the second-hand market still in great condition, proof of their commitment to excellence and attention to detail – a defining trait of this exemplary House.

"Colour is the story of our life."

Rosita Missoni

Their success took them to show in Milan from 1974, away from Florence, where they were praised internationally. In 1976 stores opened in Milan, followed by Paris, Germany, Japan and New York. As *International Herald Tribune's* fashion editor, Hebe Dorsey, put it, "The Missonis do something that only great designers can do. They have established a style and they work on it, improving it, instead of changing everything every season."

In 1997, the business was handed down to Angela Missoni, their daughter. "M Missoni" was created a year later (a new line for men and women). They launched online in 2000 and, in 2003, celebrated their fifty-year anniversary with a retrospective show featuring over one hundred striking archived looks, "with the aim of highlighting the continuity and at the same time the actuality of Missoni's language," as described on their website.

In 2022, Filippo Grazioli was appointed creative director of the brand, following Angela Missoni's retirement, and Alberto Caliri took charge of the Home Collection, under the creative supervision of founder, Rosita Missoni. Grazioli's first women's collection (for Spring/Summer 2023) was a true homage to the brand's journey – a sensual play on textures, bright colours and feminine silhouettes, featuring some of the renowned zigzag patterns that are at the heart of the brand and which define this luxury fashion house.

Milan Fashion Week

Missoni's Autumn/Winter 2023 collection, designed by Filippo Grazioli, was feminine as well as glamorous.

MOSCHINO

Founded in 1983 by Franco Moschino (1950–94), this exciting label loves to push boundaries and appropriate elements from popular culture (from McDonald's to Barbie) to create new, spectacular trends.

Having trained as a painter, Franco Moschino freelanced as an illustrator for fashion magazines and houses, and decided to enrol at the Istituto Marangoni to study fashion. When he left the school, he collaborated with Versace as an illustrator (from 1971–77) and designed for the Italian company Cadette until 1982, before creating his own label: Moschino Couture. Moschino soon became known for his distinct sense of humour, bold use of colour and prints: he was now the "one to watch" on the Italian fashion scene. "I was surprised when I became successful in Italy, very surprised," he told British *Vogue*. Diffusion lines followed – Moschino Cheap and Chic for women (1988) and Love Moschino (originally known as Moschino Jeans) from 1986–2008, for both men and women.

Sadly, Moschino died of a heart attack in 1994. He was succeeded by Rossella Jardini, his former assistant, life-long friend and right-hand woman, whose commitment to his legacy translated into huge success. She became creative director of the brand. A true creative, she told the *International Herald Tribune*: "The glossy, glamorous and cool world of fashion has never particularly fascinated me: I adore fashion and many of its representatives not for those aspects but for the creativity, the research and the effort that remains behind every collection." Jardini held the post until 2013, when designer Jeremy Scott took over for a decade, presenting his first collection in Milan for Autumn/ Winter 2014.

A Moschino "Milkshake" shoulder bag from the McDonald's capsule collection, seen here on the streets of Düsseldorf.

Under Scott, Moschino enjoyed further prosperity, enriching the international fashion scene with thought-provoking collections and a humorous twist. Although he sometimes designed showpieces that were perfect for celebrity photo-opportunities – such as Katy Perry dressed as a chandelier for the Met Gala 2019 – his wit and conceptual ideology didn't take away from the extraordinary craft behind his work. His Spring/Summer 2017 collection, for instance, was based on cut-out cardboard paper dolls, a critique of the superficial fashion industry and a social commentary on how we are coming to rely on screens and seeing the world as two-dimensional. Another collection that is still a talking point among fashionistas for its irony and humour was his Autumn/Winter 2019 presentation, inspired by *The Price Is Right* – a parody of said television programme. Here, models

Moschino's Spring/Summer 2023 show was a fun and theatrical presentation featuring many inflatable accessories.

"If you can't be elegant, at least be extravagant."

Franco Moschino

styled with a hint of a 1950s "Stepford wife" aesthetic and plenty of hairspray wore beautiful dresses with over-the-top accessories – an oversized toothpaste tube worn as a handbag, even a huge kimono, which resembled a TV dinner, complete with large carrots, peas and sweetcorn. He also designed a very "pop" collection for Spring/Summer 2023 in bright colours, styled with inflatable pool accessories (dolphin armbands, turtle and tiger floats) – as a literal social commentary on world inflation. The first model's outfit encapsulated the collection's message: an "LBD" (Little Black Dress) with an inflatable red heart, representative of Franco Moschino's quirky designs.

In 2023, Scott stepped down and, in a statement, said: "I am so proud of the legacy I am leaving behind. I would like to thank Massimo Ferretti for the honor of leading this iconic house. I would also like to thank all my fans around the world who celebrated me, my collections, and my vision, for without you none of this would be possible."

To celebrate its fortieth anniversary, a special show took place in Milan's Fashion Week in September 2023. It brought together the work of the four influential stylists: Carlyne Cerf de Dudzeele, who has collaborated with Jeremy Scott at Moschino, Katie Grand, Gabriella Karefa-Johnson and Lucia Liu, designing ten silhouettes each.

Following this presentation Davide Renne was appointed the new Creative Director of Moschino, starting 1 November 2023.

PRADA

In 1913, Mario Prada and his brother Martino founded Fratelli Prada, a leather goods shop in Milan. It was a very successful store that sold their popular Prada "Walrus" case as well as a number of imported English steamer trunks, luxurious bags, beauty cases and accessories such as umbrellas and walking sticks. By 1919 they were appointed official supplier to the Italian Royal Family and incorporated the House of Savoy coat of arms and a knotted rope design into their logo.

Mario's son had no interest in the family business: his daughter, Luisa Prada, ran it for twenty years until, in 1978, her own daughter – and Mario's youngest granddaughter – Maria Bianchi, known as Miuccia (b.1949), was asked to join them. Miuccia studied Political Science at Milan University and was preparing for an acting career when she joined the family business as accessories designer. By 1978 she had taken over the firm, transforming it from a modest luggage brand to an international luxury institution.

Miuccia met her husband, Patrizio Bertelli, in 1977 at a Milanese trade fair. He had his own leather goods company, but became one of Prada's suppliers and later the business manager, when Miuccia took over the brand. His vision was instrumental to the overall success of Prada. He advised Miuccia to discontinue importing English trunks and together, they focused on creating Prada's identity as we know it today. A turning point for Prada was the introduction of a new line of nylon accessories and backpacks, for which

Gigi Hadid models Prada's Autumn/Winter 2023: an elegant yet utilitarian collection.

The Spring/Summer 2019 Menswear Prada
collection combined sportswear and tailoring, adding
bags and oversized hats as accessories.

"Fashion is instant language."
Miuccia Prada

Miuccia decided to use water-resistant Pocono, a fabric that was in line with her industrial aesthetic. Nylon was a functional material previously used to line trunks, which had also been utilized to make tents and parachutes during the Second World War. In 1984, Miuccia Prada designed the celebrated nylon bag (the first one was called the "Vela" backpack), completely challenging tradition with her innovative and avant-garde vision. These bags were an instant bestseller, the black backpack in particular, and spoke to a younger, fresh audience. They also slotted into Miuccia's practical yet luxurious ethos, which became synonymous with the brand, especially during that decade.

In contrast to the "glam" maximalist fashion of the decade, Miuccia's vision was minimalist: simple shapes and clean lines with a focus on functionality. It was a radical and exciting time for fashion. Prada became noticed and started to expand, with the first ready-to-wear collections for women designed in the late 1980s debuting on the catwalk for Autumn/Winter 1988 and their first menswear show taking place in Spring/Summer 1998. Further lines were added: the Prada Linea Rossa denim line and Prada Sport (in 1997 and 1998), followed by Prada Eyewear in 2000.

Miu Miu, a diffusion line directed towards a younger audience, launched in 1993 and was named after Miuccia's childhood nickname. A resounding success, its brand ambassadors included Drew Barrymore, Chloë Sevigny, Katie Holmes, Kirsten Dunst and Vanessa Paradis in campaigns shot by Terry Richardson, Juergen Teller, Mario Testino and Corinne Day.

Miuccia's passion for art and creativity is an integral part of the brand's trajectory. Since 1993, Prada has organized contemporary art exhibitions, featuring artists from all over the world, and collaborated with eminent architects such as Rem Koolhaas and the Herzog & de Meuron firm to build some of their most iconic flagship stores. A permanent exhibition space, the Fondazione Prada, which includes the photographic gallery, Fondazione Prada's Observatory, opened in Milan in 2015.

A new chapter began for Prada in 2020, when Belgian designer Raf Simons (b.1968) joined the House as co-creative director with Miuccia, sharing "creative input and decision making". Their debut collection, Spring/Summer 2021, was shown (in digital format) during lockdown, as part of Milan Fashion Week. It was described by the House as a "creative conversation in progress", in a collection infused with a hint of the 1970s that included beautiful duchesse satin looks. In a very Prada twist, their first post-pandemic live show was shown simultaneously in Milan and Shanghai, with two sets of girls modelling the same looks in their respective locations. It was very well received, with plenty of black but also lime green, yellow, orange and aubergine tones: once again, Prada captured the right balance between femininity, sensuality and simply looking cool.

Prada remains a global leader and a key player in the Italian fashion scene. Miuccia, Raf and the team continue to set trends and shape the landscape within the industry with their unique ability to draw from Prada's rich, luxurious heritage and make it relevant to the present day. Without losing its distinct identity, Prada combines beautiful, super-stylish tailoring with impeccable yet quirky taste.

A delicate collection with plenty of twinsets, knee-length skirts and hooded sweatshirts came together for Miu Miu's Autumn/Winter 2023.

VALENTiNO

Born in 1932, in the Italian northern region of Lombardy, Valentino Garavani, who would be known to all simply as "Valentino", became interested in fashion at a young age, spending time with his Aunt Rosa, who owned a trimmings shop. He moved to Paris when he was 17 to study at the Chambre Syndicale de la Couture Parisienne and completed an apprenticeship with couturier Jean Dessès in 1955 before working with designer Guy Laroche for two years. He then returned to Rome, where, with the financial support of his father, he was able to open an atelier on the famed Via Condotti. After a slow start, but determined to succeed, he teamed up with architecture student Giancarlo Giammetti to launch his eponymous brand. The partnership was a match made in heaven, with Giancarlo managing the business, and in 1962, Valentino showed his first couture collection in Florence, at the Palazzo Pitti's Sala Bianca, where his work was met with overwhelming applause.

Valentino's delicate yet formidable gowns were the ideal fit for Hollywood – striking the perfect balance between classic elegance and modern charm. When Elizabeth Taylor, who was in Rome shooting the blockbuster *Cleopatra* (1963), noticed his work, she ordered a white gown, which she wore for the premiere of the movie *Spartacus* (1960). From Sophia Loren, Gina Lollobrigida, Audrey Hepburn and Jackie O (who married her second husband, Aristotle Onassis, in a Valentino gown in 1968) to Julia Roberts – who wore vintage Valentino to receive an Oscar for Best Actress in the film *Erin Brockovich* in 2001 – Valentino has always had plenty of faithful admirers.

A lilac dress took centre stage during Valentino's
Haute Couture Spring/Summer 2023 show.

"Elegance is the balance between proportion, emotion and surprise."

Valentino Garavani

His dresses became known for their femininity (bows, ruffles, lace and fine fabrics) and his trademark colour was red, ever since he attended an opera in Barcelona when he lived in Paris and worked with Dessès. The opera made such an impression on him, and he was so inspired by the costumes he saw on stage, that he always included red in his own collections, a colour which became known as "Valentino red" – *rosso Valentino*.

"I understood at that moment that, after black and white, there is no more beautiful colour," he said.

In 1967, Valentino was awarded the Neiman Marcus Award (an annual prize given to celebrated fashion houses, sometimes referred to as the Oscars of Fashion). The following year, now showing in Rome, and in contrast to the colourful fashions of the Swinging Sixties, he designed his "white" Haute Couture Spring/Summer collection in tones of ivory, beige and white. It included long skirts and delicate suits with matching embroidered jackets and became celebrated for its simplicity and exquisite craftsmanship. His graphic "V" logo was also featured for the first time.

Opposite: Valentino loved to design red dresses, as seen in his Haute Couture show of Spring/Summer 2008.

Overleaf: Valentino's Haute Couture Autumn/Winter 2022 collection was staged at Rome's Spanish Steps.

Milan Fashion Week

Then in 1969, he opened his first store in Milan, followed by one in Rome and another in New York the next year, when he launched his prêt-à-porter collections.

During the 1970s, Valentino spent a lot of time in New York with his friends Diana Vreeland (American *Vogue*'s editor-in-chief) and Andy Warhol. His collections adapted to the times with midi skirts and boots, and later to the power dressing of the 1980s. Reflecting his fun attitude and self-deprecation, in 2006 he appeared in a cameo role in the blockbuster, *The Devil Wears Prada* – starring Meryl Street as Miranda Priestly, a cut-throat fashion editor.

In October 2008, after 45 years in the business, Valentino finally decided to retire and received a standing ovation for his final show. Maria Grazia Chiuri and Pierpaolo Piccioli, who had worked together as accessory designers, took over as joint creative directors until July 2016, when Chiuri (having worked with Piccioli at Valentino for 17 years) went on to work for Dior and Piccioli stayed on as the brand's sole creative director.

Valentino's legacy lives on. As one of the romantic designers of his time he has created some of the most beautiful dresses ever seen, with exquisite taste and perfect execution. With elegance as its trademark, Valentino never ceases to take our breath away, season after season.

A stunning Valentino piece with floral detailing is modelled by Gigi Hadid for the Haute Couture Autumn/Winter show of 2019.

VERSACE

Gianni Versace (1946–97) was unquestionably one of Italy's most innovative designers, whose fearless and visionary approach was to forever change the face of fashion. Born in Reggio Calabria into a fashion family (his mother was a successful dressmaker), he studied architecture before joining her at her studio as his buyer and designer. There, he dressed Miss Italy 1970, Alda Balestra, and began a relationship with celebrity by promoting product placement, which would eventually transform the industry. "He was the first to realize the value of the celebrity in the front row, and the value of the supermodel, and put fashion on an international media platform," said Anna Wintour, American *Vogue*'s influential editor-in-chief.

Versace's career began in earnest when, in 1972, he started designing for knitwear company Florentine Flowers, after which he moved to Milan to work for Arnaldo Girombelli, who owned several labels (Genny, Complice and Callaghan). In 1978, backed by the Girombelli family, he launched his own fashion house: Gianni Versace. From the outset it was a family affair, with his brother Santo as CEO, looking after the accounts, and his sister Donatella, who left the University of Florence to join them as his right-hand woman and vice-president.

Versace's collections were unparalleled for their controversial themes and unusual use of materials. His Spring/Summer 1991 "Pop" collection, for example, brought together high and low fashion using colourful prints. "To use art in a flat way, without creative intervention, is in bad taste. I mix it up," he told *Vogue* when describing this show. He worked with The Andy Warhol Foundation to create some of his

Models Linda Evangelista, Christy Turlington, Claudia
Schiffer and Carla Bruni are photographed at The
Ritz hotel in Paris, 1991, with Gianni Versace.

most recognizable prints, including a *Vogue* cover that
was repeated throughout. Autumn/Winter 1991, another
incredible show, has been described as the moment that
defined the supermodels, when Linda Evangelista, Naomi
Campbell, Christy Turlington and Cindy Crawford walked
down the runway wearing short empire baby-doll dresses
and singing George Michael's song "Freedom! '90", having
recently featured in the star's video of the same name (1990).

The Autumn/Winter 1992 show was another turning point,
with a collection called "Miss S&M" – also known as
Versace's "bondage" show. It was so controversial that it
received mixed reviews – some fashion journalists reporting

Hugh Grant with then-girlfriend, actress Elizabeth Hurley, wearing an iconic Versace dress, attend the *Four Weddings and a Funeral* premiere in London, 1994. Grant won a Golden Globe Award for his portrayal of stammering charmer Charles.

"I think to be superficial, you have to be very profound."

Gianni Versace

that the clothes were objectifying women. Aside from structured black dresses, figure-hugging pastel gowns and American-themed looks, there was a selection of beautifully constructed "fetishistic" outfits made of leather and silk with beautiful gold buckles. More controversy ensued when, for Spring/Summer 1994, Versace designed his "Punk" collection, which was best known for an arresting dress ("that dress") held together with golden oversized safety pins with Medusa heads on them – Versace's logo. Actress Elizabeth Hurley wore it for the premiere of *Four Weddings and a Funeral* (1994), with lead star (and former boyfriend) Hugh Grant by her side, and became a household name overnight.

On July 15, 1997, devastation struck when Versace was shot dead outside Casa Casuarina, his Miami home, when returning from a walk. As the fashion world mourned, Donatella took over as creative director and later, chief creative officer, a role she still enjoys and excels at.

In her collections she has cleverly carried her brother's legacy while incorporating her own stamp. Her Spring/Summer 2018 Tribute collection, one of the most memorable fashion presentations to date, was a stunning homage that marked the twenty-year anniversary of her brother's death. The Spring/Summer 2000 tropical prints show included a green "jungle dress" that Jennifer Lopez wore to the 2000 Grammy Awards ceremony: so many people searched for it online that it crashed the internet, prompting Google to launch their Google Images search function. Twenty years later, the

Milan Fashion Week

actress appeared on the catwalk wearing a reissued version of that same dress and received a standing ovation.

A fun collaboration between Versace and Fendi – dubbed "Fendace" – took place in Milan: a pre-fall 2022 show, with Kim Jones and Silvia Venturini as "team Fendi", exchanging roles with Donatella to close Milan Fashion Week. "It's a swap rather than a collaboration and, most of all, it is done out of friendship," said Jones. The stellar event included models Amber Valletta, Kate Moss and her daughter, Lila Grace Moss Hack, Naomi Campbell, Gigi Hadid and Precious Lee, sporting fifty looks, twenty-five per designer – and it didn't disappoint the fashionistas who had been patiently waiting for the big night.

Drawing from its extraordinary savoir faire, Versace remains at the centre of Milan Fashion Week, where it has become synonymous with sexy glamour and timeless elegance. All hail Versace, one of the go-to brands for celebrity red carpet and photo opportunities.

Previous: Model Karlie Kloss walks the runway during the Atelier Versace Autumn/Winter 2015 Haute Couture show.

Opposite: Kate Moss in the Pre-Fall 2022 Fendace show, which closed Milan Fashion Week, where Donatella Versace and designers Kim Jones and Silvia Venturini from Fendi exchanged roles.

chapter 4

STREET
STYLE

ITALIAN TREND-SETTERS

A brand-new photographic genre was born when American fashion photographer Scott Schuman, the "emperor" of street style, began to document what people were wearing when out and about and publishing what he saw in his blog, *The Sartorialist,* which he founded in 2005. Having worked in fashion as a menswear director for his own showroom, he has a sharp eye for style. A recent caption on his Instagram feed reads: "In Milan every intersection, every crosswalk is a photo waiting to happen! Milano (of course)."

Many trends in today's digital age are set by an exciting blend of social media platforms, from Instagram to TikTok, belonging to savvy bloggers, actors, singers or celebrities from different disciplines, who inspire their followers through their many posts. In Italy, one such influencer is Chiara Ferragni, who currently has 29.5m followers on her Instagram account. She is the founder, chief executive and president of *The Blonde Salad*, a blog she started writing in 2009, while studying Law at Milan's Bocconi University. Aside from commenting on lifestyle, beauty and fashion, Chiara has her own clothing label, the Chiara Ferragni Collection, which started out as a footwear line in 2013 and has since grown into clothing, accessories and childrenswear (it now has four flagship stores and is sold in 300 retail spaces). She has also collaborated with many design houses – from Dior, Ermenegildo Zegna and Louis Vuitton to the more casual Benetton and Mango, among

Diletta Bonaiuti in Milan, attending DSquared2's Women's Spring/Summer 2023 collection.

Street Style

"You can never be overdressed or overeducated."

attributed to Oscar Wilde

others. Ferragni was named European ambassador of Amazon Fashion in 2016 and in 2019, she fronted a Fendi Peekaboo campaign called *#MeAndMyPeekaboo*, where she shared a birthday party Fendi had thrown for her and her family (including her dog!) with her many followers at their Roman flagship store, the Palazzo Fendi.

In her personal life Chiara is married to the rapper, singer and songwriter Federico Leonardo Lucia, known professionally as "Fedez". A star in his own right, he has also collaborated with fashion brands including Puma, Diesel, Intimissimi and Sisley to create collections that reflect his aesthetic. He was also a guest judge during the auditions for the Italian version of the television show *The X Factor* in its seventh season. His hits include "*Vorrei Ma Non Posto*" ("I'd like to but I don't"), which spent one hundred and forty-four weeks in the Italian Top 40 and "*La Dolce Vita*", together with singers Tananai and Mara Sattei, a fun pop song which in 2022 peaked to number one in the Italian singles chart.

Known as the "King of Italian rap", double platinum Italian artist Sfera Ebbasta is another street-style fixture on the Italian scene with hits including his third studio album, *Rockstar*, released by Def Jam Recordings in 2018, which became number one in the Italian albums chart, staying there for four weeks (with thirty-five million streams in its first week on Spotify). Ebbasta's fashion collaborations include capsule collections with streetwear brands Franklin & Marshall and Evisu that reflect his bold, colourful style.

Another Italian band to break internationally and represent their country is Måneskin. Formed in 2016, the rock group is made up of Damiano David (lead singer), Victoria De Angelis (bass), Thomas Raggi (guitar) and Ethan Torchio (drums). Having come second in the eleventh season of the Italian version of *The X Factor*, they represented Italy in the Eurovision Song Contest in 2021 and won the competition with their song, *"Zitti e Buoni"* (shut up and behave). They worked with celebrity stylist Nicolo "Nick" Cerioni to perfect their provocative yet stylish look.

Fashion blogger Chiara Ferragni and her husband, rap singer Fedez, attend Fendi's Spring/Summer 2019 fashion show in Milan.

HOW TO DRESS ALLA MODA

If you want to dress *alla moda,* here are some simple tips that will help you embrace elegance and achieve that legendary Milanese style, whatever your budget. As Italian style icon Giovanna Battaglia Engelbert explains, there are women who have style and those who follow fashion. Whichever category you fall into, her top tips for looking your best include "Have fun with fashion, never wear a dress that is too tight and most importantly, wear what makes you happy". Battaglia Engelbert, who is currently global creative director of Swarovski AG, started her career as a model and later worked as a stylist for *Vogue* magazine. She defines her own style as "proper", fun and glamorous.

Swarovski's Giovanna Battaglia Engelbert and editor Anna Dello Russo on their way to the Gucci Autumn/Winter 2017 fashion show in Milan.

Mix and Match "Italiano"

Sometimes, clashing prints and styles can elevate your overall look, creating a lasting impression. Fashion stylist and brand consultant Diletta Bonaiuti (owner of children's clothing company Adultiny) is well-known for her love of combining classic and modern styles and mixing feminine and masculine looks – especially when attending Fashion Week. She is particularly fond of checked blazers, which, of course, can make a great statement. More is more!

This "mixing and matching" is something we often see on the runway, especially when watching Italian designers, whose commitment to their heritage is often combined with modern cutting-edge trends or with the latest production of fabric technology. Gianni Versace, for example, was well-known for mixing concepts – classic tailoring and sportswear or what he called "high and low" fashion (successfully mixing "street" with couture); and Fendi famously explores the latest fabrics to create classic garments (for example, in the men's Autumn/Winter 2020 show, where the Fendi x Anrealage capsule collection included coats that changed colour under UV lights on the runway, simulating how they would perform in the sunlight).

Another brand that has mastered the art of making a statement by combining styles is Dolce & Gabbana. The designer duo's Spring/Summer 2021 (with the hashtag #DGSicilianPatchwork) was a beautiful expression that succeeded in bringing together seamlessly bright colours and a variety of prints. As Domenico Dolce describes in a video missive: "Given our long experience being inspired by Sicily, we wanted to tell of all that you can find on an island like this, the different cultures that dominated, from the Spanish to the Arabs [to] the Normans."

Above: Bold colours add personality on the runway of the Autumn/Winter 2022 Gucci fashion show.

Opposite: A mix of styles was seen in Dolce & Gabbana's Spring/Summer 2022 collection.

Prada's quirky style is in the detail: in the Spring/Summer
2019 show, models wore high heels with branded socks.

Key Pieces

When putting together an outfit you can often include a key item that will bring it to life. This could be a simple article of jewellery, an accessory, or a special piece of clothing. As Donatella Versace says: "Wear a fabulous smile, great jewellery and know that you are totally and utterly in control."

We find a number of significant examples in the Italian fashion world: designer Delfina Delettrez, Fendi's artistic director of jewellery (who founded her successful eponymous jewellery label in Rome in 2007), presented an "Haute Jewellery" collection (thirty pieces of Fendi precious jewels) at the Autumn/Winter 2023 couture show, where minimal garments were offset by these stunning accessories. Investing in such pieces will not only make you look fabulous, but may also be a very emotive purchase that can, in time, become a part of your identity. You can stack rings, wear asymmetrical earrings or perhaps go for a single, bold item – the choice is yours.

Another example of how a look can be transformed very simply by a key accessory was seen at Prada's Resort 2018 show. Here, Miuccia Prada dressed her models in socks and heels, adding a quirky edge (the chic librarian look) to an otherwise conservative collection. Similarly, Miu Miu's Spring/Summer 2023 show featured some stunning boxy blazers that stood out in the presentation and created a lasting and strong aesthetic. This collection also highlighted the art of layering garments in different yet complementary hues – from white to grey and beige, creating a sophisticated colour palette.

Street Style

Finishing Touches

When it comes to fashion, finishing touches are everything as they can add individuality to your overall look – something which Italians have a natural flair for.

Sunglasses – best if coloured, "to make your look more interesting," according to Bonaiuti, can be worn in retro, cat-eye, aviator, square or oversized designs. Handbags (from tote to nano) are another signature accessory, as are scarves (worn à la air hostess or as a headscarf), belts, hats (offering sun protection as well as personality) and shoes – all essential components in the quest to emulate Italian style. And whether you are going for natural beauty or an Alta Moda look, the importance of hair and make-up cannot be underestimated: a sixties smoky eye, natural lip gloss, an up-do or long hair worn in a casual ponytail.

"Fashion fades, style is eternal."
Yves Saint Laurent

A classic scent, such as the original Acqua di Parma, will complete your outfit. This cologne was created in 1916 by Baron Carlo Magnani with the help of his chemist, who wanted a fragrance to "remind him of his birthplace, family, and the Italian sun". The unisex citrus perfume, which has become synonymous with Italian luxury, contains notes of lavender, rosemary, Sicilian citrus, Bulgarian rose, jasmine, amber and light musk. It is still made in Italy, of course, and sources all its ingredients (except the patchouli) locally – *una bellissima tradizione!*

This timeless fragrance has become a symbol of Italian craftsmanship and sophisticated culture.

iNDEX

CREDITS

The publishers would like to thank the following sources for their kind permission to reproduce the pictures in this book.

Alamy: Abaca Press 62; /Allstar Picture Library Limited 56; /Cinematic 49; /Keystone Press 24; /Doug Peters 68; /PictureLux/The Hollywood Archive 40; /Pictorial Press Ltd 13; /Retro AdArchives 157; /ScreenProd/Photononstop 39; /United Archives GmbH 14

Bridgeman Images: Mondadori Portfolio 18; /Philadelphia Museum of Art, Pennsylvania, PA, USA / Gift of Mme Elsa Schiaparelli, 1969 30

Getty Images: Vanni Bassetti 118; /Dave Benett 138; /Marco Bertorello/AFP 123; /Bettmann 43; /Victor Boyko 120; /Stephane Cardinale – Corbis 31, 60; /Rosdiana Ciaravolo 89; /Stefania D'Alessandro 84; /Pietro D'aprano 81, 110, 154; /Ferda Demir 86-87; /Tiziana Fabi/AFP 94; /Fairchild Archive/Penske Media 20; /Giovanni Giannoni/WWD 32. 34. 35; /Enzo Graffeo/BIPs 97; /Jonas Gustavsson/Sipa USA 135; //Ernst Haas/Hulton Archive 37; /HGL/GC Images 102; /Taylor Hill/WireImage 106; /Derek Hudson 55; /Hulton Archive 114; /Sujit Jaiswal/AFP 64-65; /Pascal Le Segretain 140-141; /Tim Jenkins/WWD/Penske Media 46, 47; /Feng Li 101; /Marco Mantovani 67; /Emma McIntyre 7; /David Montgomery 105; /Antonio de Moraes Barros Filho/WireImage 72, 75, 130; /PAT/ARNAL/Gamma-Rapho 137; /Marc Piasecki/WireImage 129; /Jacopo Raule 70-71, 90-92, 132-133; /Justin Shin 98; /Christophe Simon/AFP 83; /Andreas Solaro/AFP 149; /John Springer Collection/CORBIS 42; /Sygma 50-51; /Venturelli/WireImage 108-109, 112, 125, 127, 142-143, 153; /Christian Vierig 150; /Victor Virgile/Gamma-Rapho 23, 77, 78, 80, 117, 152; /Peter White 59; /Sean Zanni/Getty Images for FENDI 95

Shutterstock: 147; /ANSHARP 8-9; /Kobal 15; /Olycom Spa 17; /John Rawlings/Condé Nast 29

Topfoto: United Archives 45